THE VIRGIN WAYS

A FLIGHT TO MY THOUGHTS AND EMOTIONS.

HINAL RATHOD

ISBN 978-93-5610-134-0
© HINAL RATHOD 2022
Published in India 2022 by Pencil

A brand of
One Point Six Technologies Pvt. Ltd.
123, Building J2, Shram Seva Premises,
Wadala Truck Terminal, Wadala (E)
Mumbai 400037, Maharashtra, INDIA
E connect@thepencilapp.com
W www.thepencilapp.com

Author biography

I am a 2nd year psychology student, very much interested in literature too. From early childhood I have been interested in the poetry section of literature . Wanting to express my thoughts about various aspects of life , I felt there could be no better option than poetry. I started writing poetry not only to express my thoughts but also to quote my views and describe my 'photography' , another passion of mine.

CONTENTS

Epigraph

"It's all a play of emotions ; life is a play of emotions and we all are the shadow puppets of emotions. "

Acknowledgements

I dedicate this book too my family, my teachers, my friends, relatives and all well wishers.

A very sincere and special thanks to my dearest and adorable parents, Mr. Jay P. Rathod and Mrs. Edna J. Rathod who have put in their sweat and blood in 'my growth'. I extend my heartfelt gratitude to them for always supporting me and motivating me to write better.

I also dedicate this book to my fellow readers who will surely enjoy reading my work and also be encouraged to do the same.

MYTH OF TOGETHERNESS

And one day a magician entered in her life

A totally crazy mess

When I too was in a very pain

He took the broken girl and

Lighted the lamps in her darkness

And made the most boring quarantine

A way of festive and fabricated the

Flowers of happiness

He was her Prince Charming

While she was his dream girl

And both together lead up to a

Beautiful fairy tale

Which ruled the negatives off

And brought the positive molecules

Of a bit sour and full of sweetness

Both were the strength together

And broken plucked rose when separated

While they struggled to create their fantasy love story

They constructed an epic

SPAN OF LOVE

That fathom of you
In me
As I walked alone
Feeling the darkness
And those cool wide's
Of your arms
An known fragrance
Surrounds me all the
Way back to the days
We nurtured in our nostalgia
Yet you moved on
And so did I
But still our roots
Not far apart
Just our paths apart
While we face the reality
Of being miles apart
Still a lit of being
Destined together...

STOUT-HEARTED

I am a very solved mystic
To be fathom,
Until you're wide awake of the
Taste of meh riddles
A thrill in my sight,
As the jumbles floating ,
In my life; of the hell
Flowing all lies..
As I wither man smile,
Dat fare me towards the scotch,
Once off ones head..
As if gladding the
Peace enclosed by ...
Flee out the essence of
Thine, dat connect to
The aroma of man
Rage ...

POTENTIALITY OF WITHIN

Let me lay free
As I flee
Breaking the strands,
Aspiring the freedom .
As I nourish once
The personality of my own
Smashing the rules
While cherishing my alley,
As I echo my
Conscious dat
Leads to the
Castles in the air
Of the mysteries
Of my soul
Dat steers the
Powers of universe
To make altogether.....

ARDOUR OF OUR TALE

The days dat are fragmental
Without you
As I cease for you
One glance
Dat isolated voice dat gratifies
My ears and soul
While you hold my hand
Vigouring mah veins
With the warmth of my soul
You are the world to me
And I am the life to you
As we go footing simultaneously
Maybe miles apart but still
All concurrently breaking the
Extent of notable and secret
Riddles while nurturing
Our own...

MOANA OF LIFE

High tides chasing the shores
As they connect me heartily
While I endure the gale within
That releases the pessimist anxiety
As though indulging the
Optimistic ones...
And as the night falls down the sea
Which leads to prolific
Overwhelming twilight
Of the eminence of the glister
Of its elegance
That heads my tranquillity
Into the exhilaration
Of within heaven...

SILENCE TO TOUR DE FORCE

Unspoken locution
Yet spoken
The ways I proclaim
The feelings yet unspoken
The pain once felt
Unknown to the universe
Kept aside in the
Silence of the depth
Of my psyche
Noiseless I rise
Disowning the twinge
Grasping the power
Of my richness.

ONE'S ESCAPE

I flee to feel
The nightmares felt
As I fly
Breaking the vaults of paradise
Out stretching the routes
That once obstruct
As I go across
The untraversed path
That ought to decamp
The benchmark
As I bolt to freedom
From a solitary locus to another
Backing passion of
Winning the globe

PIECE OF CHORDS

Melodies that I tune in
That gives peace to my soul...
Lyric I feel on,
Thee unspoken expression
Yet expressed...
Rendering the feels
I feel...
As the ocean waves
Flows....
The headwind
Breeze...
With the pleasing
Warmth to my
Psyche...
Tunes in the air
That refrain my psyche
With patience and aspirations..
The melodies
I tune in....

HOURS OF DARKNESS

Darkness has its
Own beauty:

You need to
Find your own
Light....
As the stars shining
In that stupefying
Darkness,
Hiding out a lot
Of mystics
Thou shining out
Aesthetic

ESPLANDE

A path to walk
Where no one has
Is far better
Than to follow
A path blindly.....
Trust yourself
More than others ......
You'll shine out to be Different....

BEAUTIFUL FLOWER

Oh beautiful flower!
Sweet is your perfume
Your colour bright
You sway in the wind
Like a child on a swing.

Oh beautiful flower!
A symbol of love
You lend a smile
To a lonely face
And a broken heart.

Oh beautiful flower!
You are nature's gift
For a beauty and grace
The best we could get
Oh beautiful flower!

BEWITCHING SPELL

A fragrance that surrounds
Day and night
That inhales all the positive vibes
And touches the river of my soul
Sweet is her anger
And spice is her nature
Both together are the perfect
Gel of the tart
Each in their ways are
The best of creators
While they get together
Are the aroma of the
Beautiful Valles
She is the scent of all the possible
Dreams ever dreamt
And just a familiar odour
Difficult to understand and hard to live without

THE SPARKLE IN MY SKY

The clouds of the happiness
I inhale in the ocean of mine
And the thunderstorms I
Exhale out of the high tides
While the lessons I've learned
All over the period and still on
Just the smile that keeps me
All time excited and enthusiastic
Just as the sun rise
As the dawn held in
Moods of frolic evenings pioneer
As it slows down to darkness
I de-stress up in tranquillity
While the midst of sky
I work out in the ways of
Enhancing the ways of glittering
The blue into divine charm of living.

PATHS UNKNOWN

The mysteries of untraveled path
To the riddles of ones
Heading towards thee
Mystic of my trail ;
Getting over thee thrill
And hiding in silence ,
Breathing thee essence of freedom
While escaping thee fragrance
Of thee transparency ;
Conquering thee fire with thee
Thunderstorms of thee ocean ,
Mainstreaming thee world
As l entering thee doors
Of my life...

HEROIC AIR

Sitting in the shadows
Abiding the pain of
A wounded who once
Had a tale of a worrier
Striving to walk off thee
Ache although leaving all hopes behind
A sparkle of motivation needed
Still the hands pulling back
To the same twinge
A hopeless feel within
Compliments thee vibes
Though the love, affection and care
Lacking behind the path
Tied with rules, customs, fake beliefs
Blocking breathe ahead
The worrier trying to gasp
While fear of the dark side
Heading towards blackness;
Merely a beam of hope enlightening
Faith of the injured
Sailing to thee battlefield with

New dreams to cherish and
A way more to life.

FIRE OF HER SOUL

She is the silence
Journey to her solitaire
A way to the extent of the universe
The more you reach the ends
More you get into the tales
Once more to be hostile
On the other at a way to savage
A closed wounded hard cover
Fragmental with the infelt of odour
A wise mind with the
Fragmented bush
And the strength to demolish
The hindrances off the way
Honeyed with poison
And a sharp edged weapon
Easy to get into, difficult to withstand
She is a mystery clubbing
The bunch of red blonde roses
As her one glance
Is the sword to hearts...

DISTANCES...

Sometimes it is just very difficult to handle certain distances ... To just let go off your only constant with whom you have seen your beautiful future ... Two souls deprived by pressure of being perfect for their own people ... Yet separated from each other ... Still hearts wandering out for the other one .... Eyes waiting to see the glance of that one particular beauty ... Arms waiting to feel each other's breaths ... While souls prompting out to stay connected side by side .... Minds loitering around in the care of the beloved ... While hearts handling hard cries to be expressed ...

An everlasting love story manifested by the souls ... A love story fabricated with torn , broken pieces of different hard, rough, smooth, silky, rich, poor, fabrics of life ... Yet the souls facing all the storms to conquer the choir of heaps by the purity of their deep affection...

JOURNEYS...

Backpacks on the back
Mind-set to explore
Butterflies wandering to see the beauty
Hearts promoting to be inspired
Pages waiting to be filled with memorials
And eyes waiting to capture memories
Breath-taking breath to breathe the tranquil of soul
And skies changing as the roads pass by
To the ultimate destination to take the final breath
For the new Journey...

HAPPY FACES

Days and nights resembling gloominess
As if skies are let on fire
And the land is overflowed by the ocean
Heart full of tears
While smiles covering the wounds
Screams heard out in the head
While firecrackers bursting out of joyous
While the faces lead out with smiles;
The souls crying and hiding the wounds.

WARMTH OF THEIR FONDNESS

It's rare when you find somebody who fits your soul like a good pair of gloves.

Seven flavours of our tempting milkshake and seven lives of our walking by together.

Cosy blankets wrapped in and around with the glittering snow-like night.

As our bond proclaim our love, we stand side by side sharing the warmth of togetherness.

Bells out ringing the joy of folks.

Life and death masters us and a wish of forever lasts in us.

JUST MY EXPLORER

On my ways of traversing
I lead to a beautiful path
Where I was pinched by the thorns
Of the way where I rested over
As to I was shedding blood by my way,
And just by there passed the charm of my life
Which healed every bit of my soul,
Maybe it was my luck or my destiny
That he became the blood in my veins .
He walked himself over the path ,
Bearing the pain just for me ,
To please my inner peace
And making my exploration a lovable one .
From then till date and much more,
I thereby got my partner of my dream
To accomplish my biggest dream.....

ACHE

What is pain??
The things that make you cry ?? NO
That makes you feel broken ?? NO
The ways you stumble?? NO
It's the thing that makes you more strong
That shows you the real and fake faces.
It's not something that can burst you,
Until you yourself feel broken.
It's something that shows the bright future,
A way of life to approach you with new chances
To live with the soul of more pleasure :-
To be who you are
And love yourself immensely.
So lighten the fire within you
To have a stupefying life ahead,
To build that powerful perspective
That no one can handle....

JUST FOR YOU...

In this galaxy is born
A brightening bloom flower
Which makes everyone smile
In and around just by glance of it
You are the inspiration to many
And the cheer of joy in silence
Be the same and love yourself
While one day you'll bloom like
One of the most aesthetic
Blossom into this world
And will shine the fragrance of yours
To the end of the universe.
Count the memors of life,
You've lived and yet to
While you accomplish your dream
To traverse the untrodden yet
The trodden ways of your life.

FROM A WANDERER'S DIARY

The calmness I feel
Within me
As the ways I
Traverse
Dat were once
walked by somebody
Also the untrodden ones
The chords of art
Which reveal the ardour
Within me
Voyage heads me
In silence yet crashes
The stillness within me
The hike moves
My soul from
Harshness of unpleasantness
to the sentiments of ecstasy
I'm the wander why ye crave
Thee richness of thee universe
As I fabricate thee volumes of
Memor all one's in livelihood!!

DAME FORTUNE

Sailing in the roar of life
Placing the odds out to make
The eve's better to rely
Pitfalls quite a lot yet
Flowing through the mysterious
One heading over the other
And waiting for their arrival
To the best day of their life
To capture the essence of
The toil and loss made
And reached out to see that
Amazeball view that was affected
By the chaos of her 'Lady luck'.

BEAUTY OF CURSE

The sun gave us light
With the fatal spot of burn
Moon gave us darkness
With the sprinklers of twilight
Still the night is blamed for
All the unpleasant homecoming
Yet the humans
Are unaware of the hell
Given to us in the
Deepest curse of
'love' , that fakes more
Than 'hate'.

JUST STAY

Covering herself with the colourful fabrics
She turned into the depths of blackness
And a shrug of white
She paced silent around the woods
And eyes floating with drops
A bliss full of emotions fluttering around
Something that could hold the madness
That lies within her
She's on her way finding the place
Where every single thing she sees
Tells her to stay .

MY HERO

A man not much recognised
Yet is the hero of my life
A person who shed his sweat for me
Just so to I could have a royal life
His sacrifices are seen
In the smallest to the biggest of choices
A person who is always in the back
As he is the backbone of ours
Through which we stand erect
He is not just a simple human being
But the living God on earth
He is the root of the beauty
And the salt to my tart
His presence is just not felt
But his absence makes it all a mess
He is the hero of my life
And our bond is the most antique of all
He is in the every breath of mine
And that's how it makes him
The most important part of mine
Love you loads, Papa.

MOON ON THE NO-MOON DAY!

I need my moon on
This on moon day ; to sit
Beside me on the top of the world
Hold me over before I fall
Scold me over my mistakes
Love me immensely when I break
Be the light
On the darkest of nights
Yet this distance leaves me speechless
In the ways I don't want to
Our bond shines out in the
Wetting of your eyes while in mine
Your possessiveness is my happiness
Your voice is just a magic to me
Our fights are my refreshments
And a chance to be more
Back to my childhood
Your smile is my strength
Its just my simply complicated path
And you are the beauty of it
As we cherish all the memors
As we walk by.

HER WAYS OF MASTERSTROKE

From the steps of being flawless
To the ways of getting perfectly imperfect
She broke her into pieces
A treasure inside her
A hope:
'Will it ever be ripped together?'
Her past menace in the background
That trouble her :
'Will she ever be out of it?'
A lob of exhaustion and disorientation
With a heavy heart she moves
'Will she ever be able to run out of it?'
The trauma she lives in
Is the ways she creates the classics out of it
The pain that is toxic
But heads a profusion of a master piece.

THE LOST GIRL

The amazing blunder of life
Where the girl lost her everything
And left to decide the things
And tried surviving for
The loss of her soul but
She had a lot of questions within
Yet knew that her life was
Hell on earth despite she acted to be alive
And embraced the broken heart
She had and wanted to live but
Was not able to battle or conquer the fight
As the wounded had swollen
All that which she had never
Thought of her life,
Will she ever get that same aesthetic smile?
Will she ever be able to heal ?
She was a broken pile of hardest storm
And had conquered a plenty of missives'
But now she was the deep rock of broken stones compiled
together which was

Blended with heart break and all of pain .
Will she ever rip of it ? Or
She will live with that gorgeous yet broken smile ever?

MYSTIC BOY

A lost heart
Yet very vibrant
Accidentally met me in the ways of path
Who made the painful hearts light up
With loads of love and joy
He was the drug of the sweetest poison
And was the free soul
Of deep river of his graceful mystics
Hidden inside his eyes and a lot
To be explored which secretly embedded with
The spark of the peace of the beloved
And the voyager on his own path
A full boom of richness of within
And an ravishing beam
Which reaches the roots
Of the banyan tree to the
Mystics of the cactus
He is the storm to conquer the world
While the peace to lives
And a warrior with success........

SCRIPT YOUR ADVENTURE

Colour the corner of your
Soul with the toxic beauty of universe
Every corner of your mind
Has the memories of these days
Well or unwell but the sourness,
Sweetness and the spice of these years
All are the life-changing experiences
Mould it in all the tinned boils
To make it one of the most
Exciting and an roller coaster ride
Before the emergence of your last breath
Make all the exotic phases
And grab over all beauty
Above and around within you
In this minutest of living.

UNREVEALED

Journey's a mess
And mess is life.
Life's a path
Where I go on
Facing ups and downs
On the way,
As I smile
Walking by,
I was once a traveller,
Unknown to my path,
Just my destination,
Leaving behind the mess,
The love, the life,
As I go,
Unrevealing the mysteries,
That once hold me behind.
But
As I go,
Creating the mysteries.

SCOTISH MIST

The gentle touch
Of rain drops,
A heavenly feel
Reliving the negativities,
Welcoming the positivity,
As it turns in
The thundershowers
Healing the unseen
Scars ,
Peaceful song, heavenly
Feel to my heart
And leaving the fragrance
Of positivity which makes
Me smile from within....

SKETCHING OUT THEIR CONNECTION

Started with an eye contact
Forwarded to friendship
Jelled into the ways of caring
Held up in feelings
Led all in understanding
And continued with possessiveness
All hurdles cleared together
Just a way walked hand in hand
Blushing to the world of fairy tales
Cherished with the most beautiful aroma
And solving the adventurous mysteries
While fabricating the memors of love
As the king and the queen created
Their castle..

TART OF MY TALE

Desires to visit once the end of the world
So that while taking the last breath
Of my beautiful life
I could recall the days of beauty
To let the time come out of time
And explore right out there the ways of memory
Self-ruling the expedition
To the discovered paths still closed back
Roads to a free hand
From the steps of neck of the woods
To the woods of untrodden mystics
Under the artistic airspaces
Just a wish to enhance the aliveness
Of my existence over the millions of years after
And passionately trend on the heals
Of manner I snap out the snapshots and
Tune in the delightful wind speeds
As I grin from ear to ear..

CHAPTERS...

Broken piece of temple enlightened
By the sunshine of the moon
On every piece of moon
Diminishing to the no-moon day
It's an never ending orbit
Embedded with pure pearls
While some with pointed stones
Leading to some unexpected destinations
Life's an expedition lead to be lived in a hope of
A heavenly sunrise leading to the
Handsome days while experiencing
The remarkable sunset and ending
With the astonishing night lights and
Wishing for the golden fortune.

LOVE

A feeling which is more to be heavenly
Most wanted and most complicated
Yet one of the best one's ...
A feeling which every creature seeks for
Luck once have it captured and preserved beautifully
While unfortunate ones experiences the most
Crippled feeling of their livelihood ...
It is destined to be separated by the love birds
Once death is on it's way it takes the extreme
Separation on its name ....
Detached by bodies yet a hope of the other one
To be alive in the souls of each other
And reaching to the journey's end together ....

SAIL THE FINAL EXIT

Life is a journey : Death is a destination
Everyone gets to live and experience both
As it is on an individual to make it or break it
To demolish oneself in the darkness
Or to enlighten the inner glory of one
To walk by it joyously or to sit aside and wait for the destination
.... All journeys are hidden with unique secrets
While all destination are led to one with unlike cause

SOUL

Embedded with spaces
Knots of deep affections
Beams of hopes within
Layered by bliss
Paths over paths
Walking over hills and oceans
To outstretch the sentiments of
Dopamine to the soul of one
Over life over heads .

OCEAN OF MERCY

Each day as I pass through the lines, craftsmanship, fragrances, broken paths, dead ends...
I feel more in depth with the divine compositions of the ravishing colours of souls ....
The beating of hearts and utter silence in the eyes of one's breath after breath exploring the ends ...
Life goes on with unexpected fears on the paths of untouched surprises placed one after another in the minutest ...

DIVINE GAL

Flying of her hairs
Be it water or air
Beauty lied her in
Her adorable eyes
An aroma of her presence
Touching the warmth of my soul
A smile on her lips
With sparkle on her face
And melting the ice by her glance
She was a mist in the woods
And magic of her journey.

LITTLE MOMENTS

Smiles fluttering around in
The hearts
While childlike spirits up in
The minds
A speed in the legs to achieve
The heights
And popping out the triumph to be
A Kid as before
As walking by towards the destination
Shared by all
Live the littles to cherish the whole
Of it's
Capture the essence of each moments
And learn
You are the sailor of your ship , live it and
Make it worthy .

REVIVE

A gentle breeze
With some fresh conviction
Colourful vibes of aurora
Sparkling in the vision
Of the juvenile
They sight to a glamorous fate
Bold to recast the psyche
For the streets ahead
Leaving behind the grey beliefs
And heading to the brighter side
Having the boldness of the
Mind-sets to let free
The divine fortune
By enriching the drive
And Outshining one's heart on,
With the extreme of lion-hearted charm

A FREE HAND

Let me breathe,
I too have dreams
Let me lead free
In the glory of skies
And under the death of the ocean
All ways broken and overloaded
With overprotection of thee
I want to live a life beyond it,
I don't want my past to
Blackmail my future
For once let me need of it,
Stop scratching the wounds
Instead heal them
By the gentle support and care of thee
I am lost within the silence
Hoping thee to come and
Steal my silence
And bring colours into my pale soul
Tears floating over
Aren't coming out,
Just to rest once in the warmth of thee

Hold my hand for one last time
And I'll conquer the world for thee..

JUST A CUP OF COFFEE

The valley of beautiful trees
Scattered all over the landscape
And a few people who blend that
Perfect seeds which further turned
Into beautiful dark brown seeds
With the most energetic aroma
The beauty in the mornings
While starting over with the
Cup of love filled and an
Aesthetic sunrise
Just adding a spoon of the
Rich well-crushed brown powder
And hot water with a bit of sugar
While just a sip of it and one
Evolves in the bounty of it
And just a smile that brings
The world's most perfect start
With a cup of love with the loved one.

IMMA

She is the beauty of my eye
She is the main ingredient of my recipe
She is the red blonde rose in my garden
She is the peace of gentle breeze
She is the soul of my house
She is the Goddess of my world
She is the blood in my veins
She is the first word I ever spelt
She is the spirit to my freedom
She is the love of my sight
She is the pupil of my eye
She is the shadow of my walk
She is the place of healing
She is the happiness to my sadness
She is the glamor of my tale
She is the queen of my fairy-tale
She is the power of my life
She is the care of my carelessness
She is the world to me and
Her blessing is the success to me
She is just an insane stupendous
Angel to me because she is the
Purest soul ever

And the livelihood of my existence
I love you a lot, IMMA.

THE BEAUTY OF THE BOOK I RESIDED IN

A very distinct cover
I dwelled into
Where I found myself
In the character of the manual
As I went on for hours
Reading the volume
It took me from the present
To a beautiful phase of my life
Where I dreamt the
Dreams I wanted to live
It was a fiction of a
Girl who was a broken piece
And then a mystery, which
Turned her soul into the fire
That changed the fiction
Into the non-fiction.

A CULTURE OF HARMONY

Once upon a time I landed
In the city of woods, earthly colours and
Broken glasses , where I
Found the silence and peace
Which made me forget
The toxic moments I lived in .
The glasses reflected the
Soberness of the city
Where humans dressed
Into the 80's and carried
A strain-less smiles
The birds chirping of the beauties
Of the nature with the downfall
Of the waters was incredibly
Pleasing too with the fins flowing .
There lived a culture of
Harmony and the pure souls
Which seemed in the
Peep of the day and twilight.

YET TO BE FOUND

Skies are on fire
So is the soul of river
Hushed a way for lies and artist
Scratching the masterpiece
There lies a silence in the every breath
Where feels the sense of pain
Which were grabbing the roots
By it's strength , as there
Were wounds on the skies of her
It looked aesthetic on the canvas .
It peeled the scars of within
Which drenched out in the future
Of hers ,
Residing the unpleasantness
Lived a beauty of mysteries
Yet to be .....

SOUND OF SUCCESS

Be so much
Powerful in life
That no power
Can break you down ....
The world I one
Of the most cruel pleasing place
Where negatives are eager
To overpower you ....
Before it leads to killing you
Bury them with noise of
Your success
And power of your positive vibe...

UNDER THE WOODS - SOULS

Some destination leads you
To crave more tours
Carve more on the
Canvas of one's own
A spirit within one
That pushes you towards
The roads unexpected
The urge within to
Live more for now
And forever

Notes

READERS CAN JOT DOWN THEIR THOUGHTS...